THE ORPHAN HEART

Restoring
True Sonship

Larry Burden
John 14:18

LARRY L. BURDEN

The Orphan Heart
© 2015 by Larry L. Burden

Published by Insight International, Inc.
contact@freshword.com
www.freshword.com
918-493-1718

ISBN: 978-1-890900-96-0
E-book ISBN: 978-1-890900-97-7

Library of Congress Control Number: 2015935100

Printed in the United States of America.

WHAT CHRISTIAN LEADERS ARE SAYING ABOUT THE ORPHAN HEART AND LARRY BURDEN

The eternal Creator God has always been Father. The second person of the Godhead has always been the Son. Therefore the essential reality in the universe is a father-son relationship.

Out from this relationship, God works His covenantal purpose to redeem mankind. Father God seeks to establish the life of His Son in His restored sons and daughters. This process requires facing and dealing with the "orphan heart" that is rampant in our modern culture. Until the "orphan heart" is healed, the believer cannot fully come into a God-given identity of sonship and daughterhood. This in turn hinders us from reaching our destiny in life.

Pastor Larry Burden exhibits and examples fathering leadership. He is well qualified to present in this volume a path for the followers of Christ to come into spiritual fullness and spiritual maturity.

This book is well written and easily read. You will be further down the road on your journey with God and you will be equipped to help others on their journey!

—Jim Hodges, President
Federation of Ministers and Churches
International
Duncanville, Texas

The Orphan Heart, by Larry Burden, so accurately identifies the number-one core problem in most societies and cultures around the world. An "orphan heart" is perhaps the deepest root cause for involvement in cults, gangs, and other alternative lifestyles. It is an inward cry for acceptance, security, purpose, family, and ... for relevance. *The Orphan Heart* not only identifies the issue, but also offers the solution. This is a must read for every leader today. I highly recommend this powerful book by Larry Burden.

—Dr. Don Crum
Leadership International

Pastor Larry hits it out of the park with his masterpiece, *The Orphan Heart*. The body of Christ has suffered from this syndrome for far too long! It is high time that we deal with this issue so that we can be healed once and for all, and then move the kingdom of God forward in an expeditious manner. Those who read this book and apply its principles will discover that they are slaves no longer, and will be able to tap into the power of God needed to fulfill their destiny.

—Brandon Burden, President
Basilea Enterprises Inc.

The Orphan Heart is a must read. Larry Burden exposes the epidemic of the fatherless in this hour. The Lord is calling sons and daughters to be released into their true identities. The revelation and practical insights in this book will empower you to express the father heart of God and walk in true sonship. As a spiritual father, Larry has impacted my life and many others with the example of biblical fatherhood.

—Jack and Marti Landis, Pastors
City Harvest Church
Cincinnati, OH

Larry Burden gives a much-needed revelation from God to the body of Christ. God's will stated in Ephesians 4 is that each member come to maturity being whole and complete, growing up into the one "perfect man." Without the knowledge of being true "sons of God," we cannot produce "mature fathers." Most of us enter into a cycle of slavery and serving, trying to earn our way to the place that has already been given to us. Many times there are wounds from our past in regards to those who stood in that place of "fathers" in our lives. It may be from parents, teachers, pastors, fellow Christians etc., and our perceptions of what we needed from them. Wounded leaders will not reflect a true image of a loving Father. Only God as our Father can truly identify who we are. We must have a revelation of who He is to truly know who we are. In chapter 4 on "Bitter Root Judgments—The Fuel," Larry presents a very important understanding of how we may have made judgments that have stunted our growth and prevented us from fully growing up, and past events in our lives. Chapter 6 entitled, "Healing the Orphan Heart" shows how "Jesus is a Savior who was willingly wounded in order that we can be healed of our wounds." The wisdom given in this book will bring understanding to the body, causing its members to grow into "mature sons" who display the glory of the Father to the body and to the world. We will enter into cycles of life and growth that bring true increase to the kingdom of God.

—Sandy Tiso
Covenant Truths

The Orphan Heart is a must read for every believer! While the heart of Christianity teaches a paradigm of sonship in Christ, much of the church today is operating from a "fatherless" mind-set. Pastor Larry Burden powerfully addresses this "orphan-heart" syndrome that works destruction in the soul of many, hindering a life of true identity, security, and purpose as God's child. Jealousy, rivalry, and competition, as well as a desperate search for approval, are common ills that plague the hearts of many believers, including church leaders. It's time to move out of this darkness and into the light of the Father's empowering love! This book will not only show you the myriad ways of how the orphan-heart operates, but also how to break its hold and live confidently as a cherished covenant son or daughter. Chapter questions will challenge and inspire you for advancing in the Father's purposes for your life. I highly recommend this book!

—J. Nicole Williamson, Founder
King's Lantern International Ministries

Larry has done the Church and our communities a noble service by making this compelling book available! *The Orphan Heart* presents the reader with five engaging things: 1) An accurate assessment of what the orphan heart has produced in individuals' lives, the church, and our nation; 2) A clear description of what the orphan heart is; 3) A precise treatment plan that if followed, will liberate the individual; 4) An inspiring story of the author's "before and after" experience, having moved from what he describes as a toxic human to now offering a road map for multitudes; and 5) Lastly, the reader is given a courageous call to redirect not only their lives, but also the course of history!

—Hope Taylor, President
International Leadership Embassy
Washington, DC

Today's world is filled with people who are searching. They are searching for meaning in life. They are searching for who they were created to be. They are searching to fill an empty place inside their hearts. Larry Burden's book, *The Orphan Heart*, brings profound answers for these troubled lives.

The Orphan Heart is a powerful resource that can be used by individuals, small groups, or for Bible studies. I highly recommend this book to anyone desiring to be part of the solution for broken lives. Neither you nor those you help will ever be the same after reading *The Orphan Heart!*

—Barbara Wentroble
President, International Breakthrough Ministries
President, Business Owners for Christ International
Author of *Prophetic Intercession, Praying with Authority, Fighting for Your Prophetic Promises, Empowered for Your Purpose*

This book is a megadose of clarity, freedom, and hope. We were amazed at the roadblocks it reveals and the cycles it explains. It gives answers that will bring tangible change.

—Marty and Kathy Gabler
SEEC Ministries International

DEDICATION

This book is dedicated to the memory and ministry of Mel and Barbara Kunau. As true spiritual parents, they shaped the lives of many sons and daughters of the faith throughout their years of devotion to the Father's kingdom. I am grateful and honored that my family is among those who have been impacted by them. May their influence, impartations, and legacy continue throughout the generations.

CONTENTS

FOREWORD

I have spent most of my adult life dealing with loved ones who suffered from an orphan syndrome. I have three grandchildren that have been added to our family through the blessing of adoption. But, they were not the first adoptees within our family. My husband, Dennis, was given up for adoption when he was born. He spent his first several months in an orphanage until he was placed into the care of Irvin and Edna Amsden as their first son. He grew up in a middle-class neighborhood surrounded by friends and extended family, was educated in the public school system where he excelled in sports, and attended weekly Sunday school and church services at a United Methodist church. An external examination of his formative years and circumstances would have brought anyone to the conclusion that Dennis had a normal life with a moderate amount of privileges and very few disadvantages.

When he was preteen, Dennis discovered that he was adopted. The revelation did not come because his parents had determined that his maturation process had made him ready for the information. Some of his neighborhood playmates, during a kid-to-kid argument, cruelly revealed the closely guarded secret. Because of his questioning, Dennis' parents affirmed that he had been adopted. The process through which my husband made the discovery wounded his soul deeply and reset the course of his life for the next few decades.

Dennis spent his young adult life sharpening his humor so that he could be included, invited, and accepted. He worked for every relational reward. He more fully developed his personal interaction style throughout his career as a salesman, where he learned to move his clients away from their objections and into agreement with his agenda. They may or may not have bought his actual product or service, but what he was really selling was his own validation and self-worth. He was always selling himself.

Every relationship was a potential reservoir from which Dennis could extract his value. He approached marriage and parenthood in the same relational pattern. He constantly extracted or withdrew validation. Yet, in the context of deep covenantal commitments and because of the amazing grace of God, our heavenly Father began to heal the deeply wounded orphan heart within my husband. With each stage of healing, he was able to gain a more true knowledge of his own worth and a more accurate appreciation of the value of the people around him. God taught Dennis to embrace his new identity as a son of God, family member, an heir of eternal rewards, and, first and foremost—as chosen and belonging.

At the age of thirty-three, God called Dennis into full-time, pastoral ministry. In the early years of his ministry, the Lord revealed that the assembly Dennis pastored would carry a special anointing for the spirit of adoption. In other words, the church would have a unique ability to gather believers and build them together into a family unit. He labored to insure that the church had a multigenerational heart so that whole family units could be embraced and welcomed into the family of God.

I labored alongside my husband as we co-pastored our assembly. Throughout the years, we have ministered to people from many walks of life and from a diversity of backgrounds. One thing we discovered was that everyone comes to Christ dragging their background with them as their own personal baggage. Identifying that baggage and unpacking those trappings is a great way to explain part of the process of sanctification. We all must remove from our souls our encumbrances or that luggage we packed from beliefs formed by a carnal and unredeemed mind. We then must repack our inner man with the truth found within the Word of God. Such is sanctification! "So get rid of all the filth and evil in your lives, and humbly accept the word God has planted in your hearts, for it has the power to save your souls" (James 1:21, NLT).

We employed counseling tools to assist believers in identifying the "filth and evil"—that carnal baggage that they packed before they came to Christ—and to aid them to "accept the Word of God"—those new beliefs that heal and save the soul. Because of Dennis' history, we were very sensitive to the baggage of broken identify that accompanied the majority of adoptees. We were able to offer hope and pathways for victory to others in similar circumstances. However, we did not identify the orphan-heart syndrome within believers who were raised by their biological parents.

Larry Burden has hit the mark as he has identified the orphan heart that can be created in children who have suffered some sort of parental rejection or disassociation even though they may not have gone through a legal process of adoption. In his new book, *The Orphan Heart,* Pastor Burden discusses how believers often carry orphan wounds from childhood relational difficulties as their baggage into their new relationships with the heavenly Father and with fellow members in the family of God. The loss sustained from a former day continues to manifest loss: loss of security, loss of trust, loss of identity, and many more losses associated with an orphan's heart.

Within the pages of *The Orphan Heart,* Larry Burden reveals not only the pathology of the problem, but also the biblical cure. Every soul cries out to be loved, accepted, and valued. When these deep longings are not met early in life, identity is jeopardized and sense of security is threatened. Larry lays out the process of healing. Each chapter is filled with revelation and application. Larry also reveals the pathway of sanctification. The reader will not only under-stand the problem, but will also be guided into practical steps to unpack the old baggage and repack the soul with the truth of God's Word. Wholeness and holiness lie ahead for the reader of *The Orphan Heart.*

—Dr. Patti Amsden, Founder/Director
Kingdom Congress of Illinois

ACKNOWLEDGMENTS

Thanks to Mary Ann Fruth for sharing her insight of the orphan heart to me at a strategic time. Your words initiated the pursuit of truth.

Special thanks to Dr. Patti Amsden for reviewing the manuscript and working with me through multiple revisions for a superior final document. Your expertise, tenacity, attention to the finest detail, and hours of labor are deeply appreciated. It was truly a labor of love. You are a precious spiritual mother and a powerful gift to the body of Christ.

INTRODUCTION

"Pastor, I know what the problem is; it is the orphan heart." This statement was quite profound to me at the time. Heretofore, I had not heard fatherlessness described in this particular terminology. I was not familiar with its dynamics. However, I was most certainly experiencing its force. Since that day, I have come to find that multitudes are suffering from this affliction of soul and are in desperate need of life-changing help to become free of its torments.

Fatherlessness has become an epidemic in our nation. In February 2014, news commentator Bill O'Reilly shared the following statistics on his television broadcast, *The O'Reilly Factor*:

- 71% of all high school dropouts come from fatherless homes.
- 75% of all adolescent patients in chemical abuse centers come from fatherless homes.
- Boys without both parents present are twice as likely to become gang members as boys with both parents present.

- 56% of all jail inmates grew up in a single-parent household or with a guardian.

These few statistics are but the tip of the iceberg; a more comprehensive list can be found at www.thefatherlessgeneration.wordpress.com/statistics. The commentator further stated that the root of poverty, crime, and despair in America is the collapse of the traditional family. Millions of children are born into chaotic homes where their parents are irresponsible or absent. I can only guess how many runaways and those targeted for sex trafficking come from broken and/or fatherless homes.

This is not too surprising since the major role of the father in the family is to establish the identity of the son and daughter. The absence of the father in the family establishes the condition for a child to become orphan-hearted.

Sadly, we, the church, are not exempt from the ills of our society and its changing culture. Neither are we immune to the fallout from fatherlessness in our own homes. We must become aware of the orphan-heart syndrome and engage wisely to shift it before it becomes entrenched in our own personality and culture. We must recognize how it insidiously finds its way into our souls and operates destructively in our daily lives. We must intervene lest we become a casualty of war to the orphan spirit.

In the pages that follow I will introduce us to the orphan heart. I will reveal how it operates and how we can make healthy changes in our mind and soul to become happy, whole, and sound again. Throughout the book I will speak about sons. Please know that this term expresses both male and female and is not gender specific.

Chapter One

THE ORPHAN HEART

For you did not receive the spirit of bondage again to fear, but you received the Spirit of adoption by whom we cry out, "Abba, Father" (Romans 8:15).

Paul's letter to the believers in Rome was meant to educate them in the basic doctrines of salvation and the general principles of the Christian life. His desire was that the followers of Jesus would put the shared truths into daily practice. He wanted the truth of fatherhood to become the foundational standard for their mind-set and conduct in life. He uses the terms *bondage* and *adoption* to explain this.

Bondage in original language is *douleia*, a term that is defined as *servitude, dependence, or the state of being a slave.* It is the state of a person in which he or she is prevented from freely possessing and enjoying a full and wholesome life. It is derived from a root word that means, *one who is in a permanent relation of servitude to another, his will altogether consumed in the will* of *another.* This is the picture of one who operates in life with an orphan heart.

In contrast to this, *adoption* in the original language is *huiothesia.* It is derived from two root words, *huios* meaning *son* and *thesia* meaning *to place.* In Scripture, to be adopted literally means to *be placed into the position of a son.* Jesus was always referred to as *Huios* in the Bible. Whenever we repent as sinners and become washed in the blood of the Lamb, we are immediately translated into the kingdom of *Huios* (Colossians 1:13) and adopted, or placed into the position of a son, in the family of God and become, "citizens with the saints and members of the household of God" (Ephesians 2:19).

While all of this dynamic transpires in the Spirit at the point of salvation, it does not mean that we immediately acquire the character and nature of the Father as a son. We are born again, placed as sons in the kingdom of the Son, and even given full covenant rights as citizens of the kingdom. However, our character and nature must be developed into that *of* a son by growing and maturing in the Spirit. This is why so many believers live shipwrecked lives. They are given the position of a son through Christ, yet continue to conduct their manner of life as an orphan. They live life under the influence and guidance of the orphan heart.

**The orphan heart is a learned behavior
that becomes entrenched in the
internal paradigm or mind-set.**

The Orphan Heart Defined

Simply stated, the orphan heart is a learned behavior that becomes entrenched in the internal paradigm or mind-set. The source of this is deep wounding that most commonly occurs from the father. These deep wounds release a host of emotions in the soul that ultimately separates the child from the identity, security, sense of destiny, and purpose that, by design, are to be instilled by the father.

In the Hebrew language, *orphan* is *yawthome,* meaning *bereaved* and *lonely.* It means *to be bereft of a parent or parents* and is the picture of a child who has lost one or both parents. Another definition of an orphan is, *one who has been deprived of a parent or parents by either death or desertion.* In the Greek, the term is *orphanos* and is translated *parentless, fatherless, and comfortless.* It figuratively speaks of one who is bereft of a teacher, guide, or guardian. In Jesus' day, it was customary for Hebrew children to have an assigned rabbi who was responsible for their training. If that rabbi were to die during the training of the child, the child was considered *orphaned* since no other rabbi would take the child to complete the training. This is why Jesus told His disciples prior to His departure that "I will not leave you orphans; I will come to you" (John 14:18). He wanted them to know that He was not leaving them orphaned!

Believers who are plagued by the orphan heart are those whose hearts are separated from acceptance, love, and security even in the presence of a church family who extends love and belonging. Their hearts are longing to belong but have the inability to do so. They have a disconnect in their souls that prevents them from engaging and trusting others. Even as followers of Christ, they are unable to acknowledge or submit to authority, instruction, or direction from the fathers and mothers of the faith who love them. Their hearts are deeply damaged by abandonment, rejection, and/or abuse from those who were supposed to love, nurture, and bless them, yet failed to do so.

What the Orphan-Hearted Look Like

Observation of orphan-hearted individuals reveals several common characteristics. First, they are ones in great pain of soul hallmarked by *loss of belonging*. Because the orphan-hearted feel lost in life, they experience isolation, loneliness, and lack of identity. There is a continual search for the answer to the basic question, "Who am I?" Without a father to establish true identity and purpose, they wander throughout life in search of true identity. They look for someone who has their perceived qualities of a father or mother and then try to emulate them. They often exhibit mannerisms, dress, and even personality traits in an effort to connect their lonely hearts to a parent figure they wish to be like.

Second, there is a *loss of value*. The orphan soul is filled with feelings of worthlessness, rejection, and sadness. This is especially true of those who have been abused or abandoned by a parent. The orphan-hearted receive the message that their lives are unimportant and their contribution to the family is neither wanted nor needed. In short, they view themselves as undesirable of those who are supposed to love them, thus producing profound sadness and a sense of insignificance.

Third, there is a *loss of security*. Rejection, abuse, and the loss of worth create intense insecurities that strike fear into the core of the orphans' souls. Peace is unseated by torment, and hopelessness takes charge of the mind-set. Orphans will always see the glass half empty and have great difficulty surrendering their souls to the Father, even when taught that He is loving, caring, and nurturing to all believers.

Fourth, there is the *loss of trust*. Orphans have been deserted by those who were supposed to love and care for them. Therefore, they purpose to never allow themselves to be hurt again by those who call themselves fathers and mothers. There is a deficit in the trust level of those in authority because of the deep wounding. Because of this, orphans will reject order, especially God-appointed order, since ultimately they see God as a tyrant taskmaster rather than a loving, caring Father.

Fifth, there is the *loss of relational capacity*. The orphan-hearted establish walls to protect themselves from further hurts and wounds. Some have an excellent ability to develop business relationships and yet short-circuit when it comes to intimacy. There is great difficulty getting close to people. They tend to keep others at arm's length and find it challenging to maintain long-term relationships. They become anxious when getting too close to people and will even sabotage their relationships in an attempt to protect from personal harm.

Orphans are very self-reliant since they are the only ones in life they deem to be trustworthy. There is little understanding to the notion that God is a provider and a shelter for their lives. Because of this, there is oftentimes an obsession with self-help. The orphan-hearted embrace self-improvement formulas in an attempt to become better, healthier people, yet rarely experience lasting change since the root issues of the damage to their souls is seldom addressed.

Authority is a four-letter word to the orphan-hearted even though deep inside there is the desire to be free of torments. They often seek affirmation and encouragement from church leaders to feel secure. However, order often equates to control. Therefore, stepping into a setting or system of order, stability, and proper alignment disquiets their souls. When love is applied to facilitate change and maturation, orphans become uncomfortable. They will often look for the flaw in leadership or church members and use it as an excuse to exit. Orphans are commonly the church hoppers that despise submission and flaunt lawless behavior within the body of Christ. They commonly claim, "I don't need you; I only need God." They remain fiercely independent and critical of any system that operates within an orderly structure.

**When orphans reach out to help others,
they are generally seeking attention
to feel good about themselves.**

Sixth, there is *loss of love and acceptance*. The need for love and acceptance within the orphan-hearted is so great that they are easy prey for ungodly soul ties. Orphans will tend to become perfectionists in order to prove their worth and so will work hard if there is a reward of recognition and affirmation. Without this, there is little motivation to serve at all. When orphans reach out to help others, they are generally seeking attention to feel good about themselves. These individuals are the ones in the church who work themselves to the bone because their work becomes their identity and gives them their sense of worth. Take them out of their job and you strip them of their identity and value.

Finally, there is the *loss of wise judgment.* Statistics reveal that 90 percent of homeless and runaway children are from fatherless homes [US DHHS, Bureau of the Census]. Many become easy prey for gangs and human trafficking. Seeking a secure environment of love and belonging, they often migrate to gangs or sex traffickers who become a surrogate family.

Orphan-hearted persons will readily pick up the offenses of others. They are very sensitive to perceived injustices and are quick to pick up on grievances against the status quo or established authority, especially God-appointed authority. In the church, they are those who often undermine or refuse to acknowledge the authority of God-appointed leadership. Their attempt to save those within the body, whom they perceive as blinded or held captive by the control of leadership, is oftentimes the circumstance that exposes their wounded heart.

QUICK REVIEW - CHAPTER ONE

1. What is the deference between bondage and adoption?

   Bondage _____.

   Adoption _____.

2. Define the orphan heart.

3. The source of one's orphan heart is _____

   _____.

4. Describe what an orphan-hearted person looks like.

5. The orphan-hearted person is in desperate search for

   _____.

Chapter Two

KNOW WHO YOU REALLY ARE

And I also say to you that you are Peter, and on this rock I will build My church, and the gates of Hades shall not prevail against it (Matthew 16:18).

In the above passage, Jesus was with His disciples in Caesarea Philippi and asked them, "Who do men say that I, the Son of Man, am?" (Matthew 16:13). They answered that many thought He was a prophet like John the Baptist, Jeremiah, or Elijah. Then Jesus asked the more poignant question, "But who do *you* say that I am?" (Matthew 16:15, emphasis added). Without hesitation, Simon answered with a two-fold revelation. First he said, "You are the Christ"; and second, he declared Jesus as "the Son of the living God" (Matthew 16:16). Jesus immediately affirmed Simon, changed his name, and declared that, "on *this* rock I will build My church…" (Matthew 16:18, emphasis added). Clearly Jesus was declaring His identity as the Messiah who was sent from the Father to deliver man from his sin, and announcing the establishment of the church. However, He was also releasing the revelation of sonship.

Rock or *petra* in the original Greek is translated *rock*, both literally and figuratively. The Hebrew word is *sur* and is the picture of a massive rock or huge boulder. Rock is used metaphorically to describe the most solid foundation upon which one can build. It speaks of enduring strength that withstands the harshest of elements. Rock is used to describe God, Himself, as the one who is reliable, trustworthy, and able to strengthen us throughout all generations. It is the picture of God who is always upright and unable to be shaken or moved by adversity of any kind. Rock also speaks of the quality of character that He gives to all his sons.

Jesus affirmed to Peter that He was indeed *the rock* of God. He was saying that He alone is the only foundation upon which the church or *ekklesia* can endure in the earth. Isaiah said it like this on behalf of the Lord GOD: "Behold, I lay in Zion a stone for a foundation, a tried stone, a precious cornerstone, a sure foundation" (Isaiah 28:16). Matthew Henry states, "Let the architect do his part ever so well; if the foundation be rotten, the building will not stand." The sure foundation is the revelation that Jesus is the Son and we, too, are sons in Him. Notice that Simon's name was changed to *Peter,* translated, *small stone* or *a piece of rock.* A piece of which rock? The Rock: Jesus, Himself! Jesus was affirming that Peter, too, was a son. Upon this revelation of sonship, Jesus said, "I will build my church, and the gates of Hades shall not prevail against it" (Matthew 16:18).

Simon's identity was forever changed when Jesus affirmed his sonship. From that day forward, this simple fisherman's life was never the same. He received a revelation that he was given a place in the Father's house alongside Jesus, Himself! No longer a mere fisherman, Peter was now a son of the living God through Jesus. He was adopted into the family and given his seat in the Father's kingdom. Whenever we see Jesus for who He really is, we see ourselves for who we really are!

We must understand the Father's plan of adoption. Paul said in Ephesians 1:4-5, "Just as he chose us in Him before the foundation of the world, that we should be holy and without blame before Him in love, having predestined us to *adoption as sons* by Jesus Christ to Himself, according to the good pleasure of His will" (emphasis added). Adoption is the Father's plan for us. He put it into motion before the foundation of time. We were seated as a son in His kingdom before the beginning of time. Love seated us and removed all shame from our past.

David said in Psalm 103:11-12, "For as the heavens are high above the earth, *so* great is His mercy toward those who fear Him; as far as the east is from west, *so* far has He removed our transgressions from us." Paul also had a lot to say on this matter. In Acts 17:28 he says, "For in Him we live and move and have our being, as also some of your own poets have said, 'For we are also His *offspring*'" (emphasis added). He writes to the church in Galatia, "But when the fullness of the time had come, God sent forth His Son, born of a woman, born under the law, to redeem those who were under the law, that we might receive the *adoption as sons*. And because *you are sons*, God has sent forth the Spirit of His Son into your hearts crying out, 'Abba, Father!' Therefore you are no longer a slave but a son, and if a son, then an *heir* of God through Christ" (Galatians 4:4-7, emphasis added).

11

In the Father's heart, we have always been His own.

There is no denying the truth of sonship in Christ! In the Father's heart, we have always been His own. He saw us and knew us before the foundation of the world, and He determined that *we* would be His sons!

Too Many Servants, Not Enough Sons

In the final two passages of scripture in the Old Testament, Malachi released a powerful prophecy. He stated that the Father would send Elijah the prophet before the great and dreadful day of the Lord. This prophet would turn the hearts of the fathers to their children and turn the hearts of the children to their fathers; otherwise, the Father would come and smite the earth with a curse (Malachi 4:5-6). Clearly this was a reference to John the Baptist. John was tasked with the assignment to usher in the Son of God. It would be this Son who would facilitate this transition into the earth. Without this shift, the curse of fatherlessness would rage as a roaring fire throughout the earth, causing major destruction to mankind and God's original design.

When I received Jesus as a young man, my understanding of Christianity was based on the assumption that I should join a church. In my mind, the church represented God. That was where people went to find out about Him. This was not altogether a faulty perception since the church is indeed the expression of the Father's kingdom on the earth. However, my first experience in church was that of service because my church placed a high premium on service. I was told that I needed to work for Jesus. So I did. As a matter of fact, I enjoyed serving in the church. To me, it was a demonstration of my gratitude to Jesus for saving my soul.

My early church experience was that of serving in any capacity that I could. I sang in the choir, served as a youth and worship minister, worked in the helps ministry as an usher and greeter, and more. When I received the call to full-time pastoral ministry, my mind-set was that of serving in any capacity that was afforded me. For years I served as a pastor, teacher, and an executive administrator in three separate churches and an international Bible school. Over the span of twenty-nine years, I was a faithful servant of the Lord; yet in that entire span of time, I never heard the message of sonship! But here is the good news. It is never too late!

Servant in Scripture is defined as a *slave, laborer, or bondman.* A servant is one who has no relational blessing of a father and who is destined to a life of servitude with no hope of inheritance. The word *son,* on the other hand, is derived from a root word meaning *build* and speaks of *a son who is a builder of the family name.* A son is one who has the relational blessing of a father with full rights of inheritance as a blood offspring. His inheritance is accompanied by assigned privileges, authority, and possessions.

When you compare a servant to a son, it looks like the following:

- Servants honor their master by working; sons honor their fathers by being sons.

- Servants build relationship by performance; sons build relationship by love and trust.

- Servants are motivated by fear of punishment or hope of reward; sons are motivated by acceptance.

- Servants are works-oriented; sons are inheritance-oriented.

- Servants strive to earn love; sons freely receive love.

- Servants fear their masters; sons love their fathers.

- Servants fear failure; sons have the freedom to fail.

Without an understanding of true sonship, generations will continue to live as orphans.

Without an understanding of true sonship, generations will continue to live as orphans. The key to remove the curse of fatherlessness is the cross of Christ. Through the sacrifice and shed blood of Jesus, mankind has been given the opportunity to enter into covenant relationship with the Father and to become sons. When we repent of our sin and receive Jesus into our hearts as our Savior and Lord, we immediately become translated into the kingdom of God (Colossians 1:13). The cross experience not only saves us from our sins, but also transforms us and provides for us a position of sonship in our Father's kingdom. Through the cross experience, we are translated into the eternal realm of the Father, where we are given a new set of lenses to view ourselves differently. We have been given the right to see ourselves as sons in the Father's house.

We Must Have Fathers in This Hour

The need for fathers in the home is critical to sons and daughters. Consider the following statistics:[1]

- 63% of youth suicides are from fatherless homes (US Dept. of Health/Census) – 5 times the average.
- 90% of all homeless and runaway children are from fatherless homes – 32 times the average.
- 85% of all children who show behavior disorders come from fatherless homes – 20 times the average (Centers for Disease Control).
- 80% of rapists with anger problems come from fatherless homes –14 times the average (*Criminal Justice & Behaviour*, Vol 14, pp 403-426).
- 71% of all high school dropouts come from fatherless homes – 9 times the average (*National Principals Association Report*).

**Fathers add to the development
of their sons and daughters by
affirming their identities, speaking into
their life purposes, and assisting them
in securing their destinies.**

---

[1] https://thefatherlessgeneration.wordpress.com

Fathers add to the development of their sons and daughters by affirming their identities, speaking into their life purposes, and assisting them in securing their destinies. Fathers provide guidance and encouragement along life's journey to help sons and daughters become successful. In the Hebrew culture, the blessing of the fathers was critical to their children. At strategic times in the child's life, the father would release a blessing that would guide that son or daughter along a life assignment. The need for fathers in the church is overwhelming. We will look at this in more detail in chapter 7.

QUICK REVIEW - CHAPTER TWO

1. What was the two-fold revelation that Simon received in Matthew 16:16?

   a. _____.

   b. _____.

2. Define the two terms *servant* and *son*.

   a. Servant_____.

   b. Son_____.

3. Complete the following comparisons of servants and sons.

   a. Servants honor their masters by _____;
      sons honor their fathers by _____.

   b. Servants build relationships by _____;
      sons by _____.

   c. Servants are _____ oriented;
      sons are _____ oriented.

   d. Servants strive to _____ love;
      sons freely _____ love.

   e. Servants are motivated by _____;
      sons are motivated by _____.

4. The need for _____
   in the church today is overwhelming.

5. How do you view yourself as a son or daughter of God?

Chapter Three

THE COVENANT
OF SONSHIP

It was right that we should make merry and be glad, for your brother was dead and is alive again, and was lost and is found (Luke 15:32).

**My identity and worth became
directly tied to what I did.**

My testimony as a new believer may be similar to many who are reading this book. When I received Christ and became born again, I joined and became a member of the local church. I became a servant in the Lord's house because I wanted to please the Lord and give something back to Him for all He had done for me. I did not realize how my work of service would soon become my identity. My identity and worth became directly tied to what I did. Whenever my service assignment changed in the church, I would go through a period of crisis. I would feel like I had failed or somehow wasn't good enough for the job. My self-worth was fragile because my identity was tied directly to my job performance. So many are like that in the church today: take away their job and you rob them of their identity. I had multiple crises as a church worker because I never realized my true identity was actually that of a son.

Jesus encountered the same thing with His disciples. He knew that they connected their identity and worth to their works. Clearly this was evident when the disciples debated among themselves about who would be greatest in the kingdom (Luke 22:24). No doubt they rehearsed all their great accomplishments as they debated the issue.

On the night of the Passover before His crucifixion, Jesus assembled the twelve disciples to partake of the Passover meal. He is quoted in Luke's Gospel as saying, "With *fervent* desire I have desired to eat this Passover with you before I suffer; for I say to you, I will no longer eat of it until it is fulfilled in the kingdom of God" (Luke 22:15-16). This was not a casual statement from Jesus. He was intensely passionate about the Passover. He could have also said it this way: "I have been waiting My entire existence to eat this meal with you." It was on that particular night that Jesus released the new covenant revelation to His disciples and inaugurated it with communion. A new covenant relationship was established that continues eternally.

The Passover was also important to Jesus because a divine shift was coming to the disciples in their relationship with the Father. In John 15:15, Jesus told His disciples, "No longer do I call you servants, for a servant does not know what his master is doing; but I have called you friends, for *all* things that I heard from My Father I have made known to you" (emphasis added). The terminology identified a relational shift from that of servant-master to one of son-father. Up to the night of the Passover, the relationship of the disciples to Jesus had been strictly business. However, after the Passover meal, that changed! In the new covenant, the disciples were no longer held by the Father as servants, but sons! That night was a divine appointment that had been in the making before the beginning of time!

The love of the Father was exponentially released to the disciples that night. They experienced the deepest love imaginable in their relationship with Christ. Their master had become their brother even as Jesus' Father had become their Father. Paul said it like this, "And because you [really] are [His] sons, God has sent the [Holy] Spirit of His Son into our hearts, crying, Abba (Father)! Father! Therefore you are no longer a slave (bond servant) but a son; and if a son, then [it follows that you are] an heir by the aid of God, *through Christ*" (Galatians 4:6-7, AMP).

The Strength of Covenant Sonship

In Luke 15:11-32, we read the story of the prodigal son. The story is about two brothers and a father. The younger brother was confused and had a wayward spirit. He asked his father for his inheritance, and in response, the father gave it to him. The younger brother took off from home, traveled far away, and immediately squandered his inheritance on wine and women. Before long, he was broke and took a job feeding pigs in order to survive. He became so destitute that even the pig feed began to look good to him.

In the midst of this horrible mess, the son came to his senses and remembered his father. He recalled that even his father's servants had enough to eat and a better work environment than he did. So he decided to return home, repent of his sins, and ask his father to hire him as a servant. In the son's shameful heart he said, "I am no longer worthy to be called your son" (verse 19). It is important to note that in his destitute state, the son knew the true character of his father. The son had a history with his father. He knew his father's nature; and in the son's deep despair, he knew that if he were repentant, his father would likely receive him and give him a job.

When the son returned home to seek mercy and ask his father for a job, the father offered him something much better—a home.

When the son returned home to seek mercy and ask his father for a job, the father offered him something much better—a home. While the son was yet a great distance from his father's house, the father saw the son walking toward home. This suggests that the father kept a daily vigil, hoping for the moment that his son would return. As his son approached from afar, the father was moved with deep compassion and ran to meet him. The father embraced his son, hugged his neck, and kissed him even before the son had a chance to say one word. The father did not rebuke his son nor demand an explanation of his son's whereabouts. The father simply opened his heart and arms and welcomed the lad home!

Not only did this father embrace his wayward son, but he also reaffirmed to the young man the honor of sonship. He first summoned his servants to bring his best robe and put it over the son, symbolizing his covering and blessing. He then placed his ring upon the son's finger, symbolizing both his covenant with his son and confirmation of the young man's renewed authority. He then called for shoes to be placed on his son's feet, symbolizing protection and a renewed ability to walk out his ordained destiny. Instead of rebuking his son, the father blessed him and restored to him the full rights and privileges of covenant sonship!

If that were not enough, the father further called for the fatted calf to be slaughtered and a feast be made to celebrate his son's return. He said, "For my son was dead and now is alive again; he was lost and is found. And they began to be merry" (verse 24). Now *that* is a true father!

The Older Brother

It is important to note that when the younger son asked for his inheritance, the father gave both sons their inheritance. By law, the older brother was to receive a double portion. We know that the younger son blew his inheritance, but what about the older brother? He obviously let the father keep it for him because the story goes on to say that the older brother was working in the fields when the prodigal returned home.

The older brother heard the noise of a celebration going on at home, and he asked one of the servants what was happening. When he learned of his brother's return and the ensuing celebration, he became very angry. He confronted his father, disturbed that in all the years that he had worked for his father there was never a party given for him. It is unfortunate that the older brother was a son by birth, but an orphan by paradigm. Even though he was a son, he had no understanding of what it meant to be a son. He merely worked in his father's field as a laborer along with the other servants in order to earn his father's favor. He was performing in order that he could gain the acceptance of his father. He had no idea that the heart of his father held this sentiment: "*All* that I have is *yours*" (verse 31, emphasis added).

The older son is the picture of the majority of churchgoers today. He represents the religious system of servanthood that is aimed at getting the approval of the Father in heaven but has no true heart connection with the Father at all. Rather than seeking the Father, churchgoers become caught up in the paradigm of the church system. When a need then arises, they expect the church to provide for that need. When the church fails to measure up to their expectations, these church people blame those in the church system who represent God and abandon that system in search of a different church that promises to do better. Their view of life becomes skewed and full of resentment toward those who wear the robe, the ring, and the shoes of true sonship. These individuals are like the older brother who refused to receive his inheritance, choosing rather to earn it. They are orphans seeking genuine identity and purpose in life but never finding it.

Years ago, I conducted a funeral service for a fine Christian man. He was a faithful believer and a good moral man. Before he passed away, he looked at his wife and said, "I hope I was good enough to make it in." He was referring to his acceptance into heaven. While his words were those of true humility, I immediately saw the orphan heart in this precious man. We have to know that none of us is good enough to be received into the Father's kingdom. As sweet as they sounded, his words reflected both the error of his understanding and the flaw in the church system that promoted and supported his orphan mind-set.

Our kingdom service is the reflection of our love for Him as sons!

We are not received by the Father because of our goodness and kind deeds. We are received because we have been granted sonship through our repentance and acceptance of Jesus Christ as Lord and Savior. The works that we do as sons and daughters are not to gain favor with God or to prove that we are worthy of His love and favor. Our kingdom service is the reflection of our love for Him as sons!

We must come to an understanding of covenant sonship through Christ. We must don the robe, wear the ring, and put on the shoes given us by our Father. We must demonstrate to the world and the church the reality of true sonship so that generations to come will not live as orphans.

The Kingdom of God Is Reserved for Covenant Sons

The kingdom of God is reserved for sons. While sonship is bestowed, it must also be developed. Even Jesus had to go through levels of growth to attain maturity. First, He was a *babe.* In Luke 2:11-12, the angels tell the shepherds, "For there is born to you this day in the city of David a Savior, who is Christ the Lord. And this *will be* the sign to you: You will find the Babe wrapped in swaddling cloths, lying in a manger." The word, *babe* is translated *newborn* and is derived from a root word meaning, *to feed and nourish frequently.* This idea is consistent with that of newborn believers who must be nurtured and constantly fed in order to keep them spiritually viable and to insure progressive spiritual growth in the early years of walking with the Lord.

Second, the Bible describes Jesus as a *child.* Luke 2:40 states, "And the Child grew and became strong in spirit, filled with wisdom; and the grace of God was upon Him." *Child* in this verse is translated *paheedion,* meaning *half-grown boy or girl* or *young child.* So while Jesus was in the process of natural and spiritual growth, He had not yet grown into full maturity. During this time, He was developing the wisdom and strength of spirit that required the work of grace. This is the picture of believers who are not yet mature but are in the process of becoming so. It is a time of spiritual growth where wisdom is key and grace must be abundant.

Third, Scripture reveals Jesus as a Son. On the day John the Baptist baptized Him in the Jordan River, the Father pronounced the blessing of sonship upon Jesus with these words, "You are My beloved Son; in You I am well pleased" (Luke 3:22). Before the foundation of the world, Jesus was destined to be the Son of God and the Son of Man. Isaiah declared prophetically in Isaiah 9:6, "For unto us a Child is born, unto us a Son is given; and the government will be upon His shoulder. And His name will be called Wonderful, Counselor, Mighty God, Everlasting Father, Prince of Peace." Note that this word *son* in Hebrew is *ben* and is translated *builder, as one who builds the family name.* It is the equivalent of *huios* in the Greek. Jesus was destined as the Son who would build His Father's kingdom in earth.

Jesus was the promised seed of Abraham and the promised King who would sit upon the throne of David. Yet, even as the Father's only begotten Son, He still had to grow up and develop into a mature Son in order to fulfill His kingdom destiny. This was not because He was lacking in any area of life, but rather so that He might identify with our humanity and establish the pattern for our growth and maturity as sons of God.

If we are going to operate effectively in our Father's kingdom, we, the church, *must grow up*!

If we are going to operate effectively in our Father's kingdom, we, the church, *must grow up*! In Paul's letter to the Corinthian church, he laments that they were too immature in their spiritual growth to receive strong instruction. He says to them, "I fed you with milk, not solid food, for you were not yet strong enough [to be ready for it]; but *even yet* you are not strong enough [to be ready for it]. For you are *still* [unspiritual, having the nature] of the flesh [under the control of ordinary impulses]. For as long as [there are] envying and jealousy *and* wrangling and factions among you, are you not unspiritual *and* of the flesh, behaving yourselves after a human standard *and* like mere (unchanged) men?" (1 Corinthians 3:2-3, AMP, emphasis added). Paul was concerned that these believers had not grown in maturity and therefore had become stuck in an immature state. There are too many just like these Corinthians in the body of Christ today. They exhibit narcissistic and entitlement mentalities that are no different from the world system.

The writer of Hebrews also had something to say about the need to mature:

Although He (*Jesus*) was a Son, He learned [active, special] obedience through what He suffered and, [His completed experience] making Him perfectly [equipped], He became the Author *and* Source of eternal salvation to all those who give heed *and* obey Him, being designated *and* recognized *and* saluted by God as High Priest after the order (with the rank) of Melchizedek. Concerning this we have much to say which is hard to explain, since you have become dull in your [spiritual] hearing *and* sluggish [even slothful in achieving spiritual insight]. For even though by this time you ought to be teaching others, you actually need someone to teach you over again the very first principles of God's Word. You have come to need milk, not solid food. For everyone who continues to feed on milk is obviously inexperienced *and* unskilled in the doctrine of righteousness (of conformity to the divine will in purpose, thought, and action), for he is a mere *infant* [not able to talk yet]! But solid food is for full-grown men, for those whose senses *and* mental faculties are trained by practice to discriminate *and* distinguish between what is morally good *and* noble and what is evil *and* contrary either to divine or human law. (Hebrews 5:8-14, AMP, emphasis added).

In short, the writer was admonishing the believers to *grow up!*

Is it any wonder that we have such a desperate need within the church for mature fathers of the faith? The deficit of true spiritual parenting has fostered the unrestricted operation of the orphan heart in the church and among the generations.

QUICK REVIEW – CHAPTER THREE

1. Why was Jesus so passionate about sharing the Passover with His disciples before being crucified?

2. Describe the symbolism of the articles given the prodigal son by his father.

   a. Best robe _____.

   b. The ring _____.

   c. The shoes _____.

3. Why was the older brother so upset with the father's response to the return of the prodigal son?

4. What three phases do we pass through as we grow into mature sonship?

   a. _____

   b. _____

   c. _____

5. The Hebrew word for *son* is *ben.* It is translated, _____
_____.

Chapter Four

Bitter Root Judgments—The Fuel

See to it that no one fails to obtain the grace of God; that no "root of bitterness" springs up and causes trouble, and by it many become defiled (Hebrews 12:15, ESV).

The Hebrew writer instructs us that we are to follow peace with all men as well as holiness, "without which no one will see the Lord" (Hebrews 12:14). *Peace* is defined as *untroubled, undisturbed well-being* in the Greek; but a more accurate translation is *to destroy all the authority that binds us to chaos*. *Holiness* in the original Greek is *hagiasmos* and is translated *purity*. It speaks of giving the Father full rights to our lives and exhibiting His behavior in our day-to-day lives in such a manner that our behavior is the direct reflection of the purity of His nature and character. Paul describes this in Ephesians 1:23 as "the fullness of Him who fills all in all." Holiness, then, is a reflection of how much of the Father actually is alive within and operational through us. Holiness is an absolute work of God's grace. By the same token, full surrender of all rights to our lives is also a work of grace.

Bitterness begins as a seed, takes root over time, and eventually springs forth into full-blown defilement that affects not only us, but also those around us.

The great tragedy of our day is that many of us have failed in this grace. We have fallen prey to offense, and rather than follow after peace, we have chosen the path of bitterness. Bitterness begins as a seed, takes root over time, and eventually springs forth into full-blown defilement that affects not only us, but also those around us.

Bitter Roots Defined

Bitter roots are defined as *sinful reactions to painful events*. The events, themselves, do not cause the root. The reaction to the events is at the core of the bitter root. Bitter roots express themselves as condemning judgments of people or the refusal or inability to forgive those who have hurt us. They manifest as names or careless words that we have either thought about, called others, or said about the ones who have hurt us. They are powerful toxic pollutants that damage and defile our souls and others around us as well. In response to hurts, wounds, or painful events, we express condemning judgments.

These judgments become bitter seeds in the soul. We may try to push down the hurts, rationalize them, blow them off, or simply just pass them off as no big deals. But they *are* big deals! These seeds of bitterness will remain intact and grow unnoticed in the soul. Over time, they will build a root system and, if left unchecked, become the driving force of our personality, manifesting such things as cynicism, criticalness, apathy, negativity, and more.

Years ago I wrote a chapter in a nursing textbook about a disease of the heart called infective endocarditis. It is an infection of the heart caused by certain bacteria that attach to the leaflets of the heart valves. Heart valves are essential to maintain the forward movement of blood from the heart (the body's pump) to all parts of the body. Proper valve function is necessary to maintain a healthy life. When bacteria attach themselves to the valve leaflets, they slowly grow and multiply largely undetected by the person or physician. The signs of the disease are subtle and only come to light after the bacteria grow and damage the valves. Because of this, normal blood flow is impeded through the heart, lungs, and all parts of the body. Without swift intervention, the person will ultimately die.

Bitter roots are much like these bacteria to the human soul. Seeds of bitterness can lie unnoticed in the soul for years, and yet they are like a fulminating infection. They slowly grow undetected; but then one day, they come to light through bitter words and the classic picture of the orphan heart. When bitterness has become so entrenched in the person's soul, their entire life has become tainted; and those around them, whom they love the most, become tainted as well! They end up viewing people, church, and even God through a lens of their soul that has become clouded by this root of bitterness. Their words ignite raging firestorms of destruction as they spew the venom of bitterness from their diseased soul toward others.

The Picture of Bitter Roots

My dad was the product of a fatherless home. His father passed away when he was just a child. He, his mother, and his siblings actually lived with Dad's older sister and her husband, both wonderful people. I know few details of the family except that they went through the years of the Great Depression as farm workers. There was little in the way of food or material goods for anyone in those days, and it was not a happy time for my dad's family.

As a child, I remember Dad being bigger than life. He was a "man's man." I enjoyed spending time with him, especially hunting and playing baseball. He was an austere man of few words and a minimal display of love or affection. He was quick to correct and pull a belt to enforce his discipline. Apparently, I was in need of both quite often. He had been given the responsibility to secure my identity and future, but he had no insight that such a thing was an important part of fathering. My relationship with him was one of love and fear, along with an intense need to earn his love and affirmation.

While I loved Dad and had a deep respect for him, I feared him greatly, which created deep insecurities and self-image issues throughout a large portion of my life. The rejection I felt from my dad fueled my lack of identity and purpose in life. I tried desperately to hide my deep fear and anxiety from others. I also exhibited a performance behavior whereby I sought success tirelessly to prove my worth and value as a person. My orphan heart struggled with my identity, my purpose in life, and my self-worth.

Even though I loved Dad, I rejected him in my heart as my father. I deemed him unfit and searched for other "fathers" who would accept me, love me, and value me as a person. I failed to realize, however, that in so doing I had passed a condemning judgment against him. This judgment became a seed of bitterness that took root in my soul and lay under the radar for years. As I grew into manhood, I received Jesus as my Savior, became a faithful church member, married my high school sweetheart, had two great sons, and engaged in a career that afforded a comfortable living for my family. Life was good!

The very things I rejected and despised in my own father were the things I found myself becoming as a father.

Except life wasn't that good. The fears, insecurities, lack of self-worth and value, and all the other hidden toxins in my soul still remained. The very things I rejected and despised in my own father were the things I found myself becoming as a father. I was austere, a man of few words, and a strong disciplinarian to fear. In short, I displayed an abusive behavior that, in some ways, was worse than Dad's! The bitter-root judgments that I made against him had surfaced in full bloom, not only defiling me, but also my precious wife and two sons, whom I loved the most.

Bitter Roots *Must* Be Removed

I can tell you that the only way to deal with a bitter root is to cut it. You cannot kill a tree by picking its fruit off the limbs; you have to kill the root. Likewise, you cannot remove a bitter root by counseling and medicating it; you must cut it! I was born again, Spirit filled, a faithful servant in the church, a good provider for my family, and a serving citizen in my community. I was also a toxic human to live with at home! I was full of fear and anger, and I was terrified of failing and being abandoned. Everything in my life had to be perfect, especially my wife and sons!

Thank God for the day that I crashed and burned. Realizing that I was a miserable failure in life, I asked God to take my life. Rather than do so, He directed me to return to the point in time where I passed the bitter judgments against my dad. He revealed to me that I had to repent of those judgments and ask his forgiveness. He did not condone my father's behavior even as He did not condone mine. Yet I was required of the Father to stand over Dad's grave and repent of my condemning judgments against him as well as ask his forgiveness. As I did, I felt the ax cut the root of the bitterness in my soul. John the Baptist preached the message of bearing fruit worthy of repentance saying, "and even now the ax is laid to the root of the trees" (Luke 3:9). By the power of God, I was liberated from a bitter soul.

The change that came over me was immediate. The chaos within my soul lifted in a moment of time as the peace of God arose in its stead. I was a changed man. I suddenly became considerate and nice. Even my wife was startled by the sudden change. She actually became frightened. I was not the same man she had married, but soon she realized the peace of God that was in me. The Father had removed all the bitterness of my soul that had kept me bound to chaos. He aligned my soul with His fullness, His holiness. He balanced the scales of my soul. He cleansed my lens so that I could see clearly and cleanly. He washed me and made me whole again! How many ways can I describe how He set me free!

Through that experience, I realized the reality of Isaiah 61:1-2: "The Spirit of the Lord God *is* upon Me, because the Lord has anointed Me to preach good tidings to the poor; He has sent me to heal the brokenhearted, to proclaim liberty to the captives, and the opening of the prison to *those who are* bound; to proclaim the acceptable year of the Lord, and the day of vengeance of our God; to comfort all who mourn." When the Holy Spirit cut that root, my prison door opened and I was released from my own captivity. I was a prisoner of my own device. My heart was broken. It was full of bitterness and defiled many people around me. I could not pray it away, reason it away, counsel it away, or medicate it enough to kill the pain. Only repentance and forgiveness would cut the root and destroy the bitter tree.

A Story to Remember

Consider the following true story:

There was a young woman who, during her high school years, lost her mother. Her dad and older brothers were alcoholics. In order to keep the family together, this girl quit school, went to work to support the family, took care of the house, and became the responsible party of the household. During this time in her life, she passed a judgment in her heart that, "men are useless drunkards who will not work and have to be taken care of." When she became old enough, she sought marriage so that she could leave home. She married a man who had somewhat of a problem with alcohol; but as soon as they married, his problem grew worse, to the point that he lost his job. Because he was out of work, the girl went to work and once again had to take care of an alcoholic who would not work, only this time it was her husband. Her judgment of men was reinforced once again.

The girl divorced this man and subsequently married her second husband. He, too, had an alcohol problem at an earlier time in his life but had been sober for a long time. He also had a stable job. Soon after marriage, this husband suddenly lost his job. Out of distress, he relapsed and started drinking again. Soon after, the girl once again had to work to support an alcoholic husband who would not work. She divorced him too! She continued to adhere to her judgment of men as useless drunkards who would not work and had to be taken care of.

Following a short period, this girl met a third man who never drank alcohol in his life. He had worked the same job for many years and was the picture of stability. She married him. After a few years of living with his new wife, this man began to drink. And you guessed it—he subsequently lost his job, too. Once more the girl found herself supporting an alcoholic husband who would not work. Now her judgment of men was forever sealed in the depths of her soul.

Were these marriage failures mere coincidences or did bitter-root judgments play a role in the destruction of the marriage relationships? Was this girl a contributor to the poor behaviors of her husbands? If there had been an intervention in her life, would we be looking at a different life story? We will never know. However, it is clear that the bitter root, seeded into her when she took care of her alcoholic father and brothers, had a negative influence upon each of her marriage relationships. I believe that her bitterness of soul affected the men she married, even defiling the one man who never drank a day in his life and had a stable job. I also believe that the tragedies of her failed marriages could have been avoided had she been made aware of the deadly force of bitter-root judgments. An intervention could have made all the difference in her life and those whom she loved.

I cannot tell you how important it is that we examine the fruit of our lives and be courageous enough to face our areas of bitterness by repenting and releasing forgiveness. This action makes all the difference between a healthy soul or a lifetime of bitterness, cynicism, jealousy, hatred, and ultimate destruction. We have the opportunity to change our future by addressing these issues in our own lives today.

Jesus did it for me. He will do it for all of us!

QUICK REVIEW – CHAPTER FOUR

1. Define bitter roots.

2. Bitter roots express themselves as _____
   _____ of people.

3. List four manifestations of bitter-root judgments in our
   lives.

   a. _____

   b. _____

   c. _____

   d. _____

4. The only way to remove a bitter root from our soul is to
   _____.

5. Removing bitter roots from our souls is through _____
   _____ and _____.

Chapter Five

THE GLORY OF SONSHIP

**But as many as received Him, to them He gave the
right to become children of God, to those who believe
in His name (John 1:12).**

Of all the followers of Jesus during His earthly ministry,
there was only one for whom Jesus declared a deep, abiding
love. That was John. He was the one disciple who had a true
revelation of the glory of Jesus' sonship. He was the one who
said of Jesus, "and we beheld His *glory*, the *glory* as of the only
begotten of the Father, full of grace and truth" (John 1:14,
emphasis added). In verse 12, the word *children* in the original language is *teknon,* speaking of children in the literal or
figurative sense. Jesus, however, is never spoken of as *Teknon*
in Scripture except by His mother, Mary. To her, Jesus was her
Child. All other Scripture references of Jesus refer to Him as
the *Son* or *Huios,* denoting His character and mature nature,
which was a reflection of His Father. He was Mary's *Teknon*
but the Father's *Huios.*

Paul states in Romans 8:19 that the earth is groaning for the manifestation of the sons or *huios* of God. While we enter the kingdom of God as children, we are not to remain children. We are admonished to grow and mature into genuine sons. Furthermore, we are to grow in the glory of His sonship as we are transformed into the image and likeness of the Son of God, Himself (Romans 8:29). The Western church fosters entertainment over transformation—an environment that lends itself to servants rather than sons. We need more mature sons!

John said that the disciples "beheld His glory, the glory as of the only begotten of the Father" (John 1:14). Glory describes the appearance, form, or aspect of a person that catches our attention and commands our recognition. All created things have been given a unique expression of the Father's glory. Just as the sun, moon, and stars have a unique glory of God, so man has the unique glory of the Son. John beheld the person of Jesus and perceived the glory of His sonship. It commanded John's recognition; and as he gazed upon this man he could only conclude one thing: This is the Son of God! For us to become true sons of God, we also must have a revelation of the glory of sonship.

The Kingdom of God and the Glory of the Son

The kingdom of God is all about the glory of the Son. Colossians 1:13 teaches that we have been delivered from the "power of darkness and conveyed into the kingdom of the Son of His love." When we receive Christ as our Savior, we are immediately translated into the kingdom of the Son and seated at the table of the Lord. We are also given immediate access to the eternal realm of the Son. When we behold Him, it commands our recognition that He is the glorious Son of the living God.

As a Son, Jesus shared and demonstrated the truth of His glory. He spoke the truth of His Father and exercised the Father's authority. He shared the gospel of the Father's kingdom and demonstrated its power. He followed all that the Father revealed to Him and released the eternal kingdom into the temporal world. He completely fulfilled His mission as the Son of glory. He reigned as a ruling King in the earth and released His Father's kingdom dominion to all who would respond. This is the *glory* that Jesus manifested in His earthly ministry.

The Father has purposed that the glory of His Son is to reign today through us. We are not only to be carriers, but also releasers of His glory. Paul said it like this in Romans 5:17: "For if by one man's offense death reigned through the one, much more those who receive abundance of grace and of the gift of righteousness will reign in life through the One, Jesus Christ." The words *reign in life* are literally translated, *reign in this life*. The glory of the Son is a reigning and governing glory that is to be manifested now through us, the sons of the living God. We are given the charge to change those around us by releasing His glory that lives within us.

We have been ordained by the Father to reign, to rule, and to have dominion in the earth *now* through the manifestation of the glory of the Son who lives inside us.

My friend, Simon Purvis, states, "The reigning presence of God is the kingdom of God." We have been ordained by the Father to reign, to rule, and to have dominion in the earth *now* through the manifestation of the glory of the Son who lives inside us. That is the glory of sonship. It first begins when we allow the glory of the Son to have full rights to our hearts, souls, and minds. The glory then flows through us to touch and change the lives of others and ultimately reshape the culture around us. It is a work completely of the Son. Christ in us is indeed the hope of His glory (Colossians 1:27, paraphrased).

Kiss the Son

No king in history compared to David. He was recorded as "a man after (God's) own heart" (Acts 13:22). Besides King Jesus, David was the greatest king to ever live. His premiere attribute was having a revelation of the glory of the Lord. No one compared to David in his ability to worship and seek the face of the Lord. His strength in worship enabled him to govern righteously in the earth. David penned the following in Psalm 2:10-12: "Now therefore, be wise, O kings; be instructed, you judges of the earth. Serve the Lord with fear, and rejoice with trembling. Kiss the Son, lest He be angry, and you perish in the way, when His wrath is kindled but a little. Blessed *are* all those who put their trust in Him."

To *kiss the son* is a metaphor that means to respect, honor, and pay homage to one who is superior. In ancient times, one would literally kiss a king's feet to demonstrate honor. Proverbs 24:26 states, "An honest answer is like a kiss on the lips" (NIV). To kiss the Son is to demonstrate the highest respect and honor to the Son of glory. It is an expression of our covenant union with Jesus. It also expresses that we are partakers of His glory. We receive Him unto ourselves and grow relationally with Him. We surrender our character and nature to Him and, thereby, share His kingly authority and display the glory of His sonship as true sons.

Years ago, I worked for a cardiologist named Thomas Smitherman at the VA Medical Center in Dallas. Not only was he a brilliant physician and medical researcher, but he was also a man of excellence in his manner of life. I began working for him in a business relationship as a research nurse, only to depart from him as a friend and admirer once the research project was completed. Through the years that I served with Dr. Smitherman, I closely studied how he conducted himself as a physician and a person. I could tell what he was thinking about any given matter at any given time. I grew to love him as a person and emulate him as a role model. Because I represented him in the medical center, it was important to me to be a reflection of his nature and character. Over time I grew in maturity to the point where I carried a weight of his authority simply because I represented him as his associate and knew him so intimately. When he needed something for our research project, I could easily obtain it because everyone in the VA Medical Center knew whom I represented. I also learned never to misuse this blessing for personal gain.

While servants are given permission to speak for their masters, sons are given the authority to legislate the heart of the Father.

This time in my life revealed to me how we are to walk with the Son. Our walk represents a covenant union where we begin relationally as servants and grow into the true character and nature of the Son Himself. We transform into ambassadors who represent the Son of glory as a son. While servants are given permission to speak for their masters, sons are given the authority to legislate the heart of the Father. Sons not only know the Word, they also know the ways of the Father. Sons carry the full weight of the Father's authority to attain all that He desires yet realize that this power must never be abused.

As I mentioned earlier, we have been given a seat at the Lord's Table. We have been given access to the Father's throne. We have been given the covenant right to grow into full maturity as a son and become true ambassadors to carry the full weight of the authority and power of the Son. The purpose of our roles as ambassadors is to effect righteous change in the world where we are to shine as lights to lost humanity. The Father has kept nothing back from us; we have all that is needed to become a Son of His glory. We are not waiting on Him; He is waiting on us!

QUICK REVIEW – CHAPTER FIVE

1. To grow into the glory of sonship means to be

   _____

   _____.

2. *Glory* is describe as _____

   _____.

3. What does it mean to *"kiss the Son"*?

4. Walking with the Son represents a _____
   _____ whereby we begin as servants and grow
   into the true character and nature of the Son, Himself.

5. Sons not only know the _____
   of God, but also His _____.

Chapter Six

HEALING THE
ORPHAN HEART

**For in Him we live and move and have our being, as
also some of your own poets have said, "For we are
also His offspring" (Acts 17:28).**

In Paul's message on Mars Hill, he makes a profound
statement that covenant followers of Jesus are His *offspring*.
The Greek term for *offspring* is *genos*, from which we derive
the word *gene*, and it is literally translated *stock*. It speaks of
the family line, generational line, and DNA. In short, Paul is
saying that covenant believers have been placed into the royal
family of the Father and have the same spiritual DNA as that
of the Son, Himself. So, while we are not the Son of God,
Jesus, we have the same spiritual DNA as the Son, Jesus. As a
son in Christ, we are instructed to live our natural lives with
a clear understanding that we belong to the family of the Son,
Jesus, and that we have the same rights and privileges as a
member of the family, just like the Son, Jesus.

For over fourteen years, I have been heralding the message of the kingdom of God. It has always been and will continue to be the true message of the gospel. The message of the kingdom includes the gospel of salvation but much more. It is encapsulated by Colossians 1:13-14 (AMP), which states that as believers in Jesus Christ, "[The Father] has delivered *and* drawn us to Himself out of the control *and* the dominion of darkness and has transferred us into the kingdom of the Son of His love, in Whom we have our redemption *through His blood*, [which means] the forgiveness of our sins." This is the message of the gospel of the kingdom in its simplest form, and it manifests through us as His offspring in the faith.

Too Many Orphans in the Church

I have made three important observations regarding the orphan heart. First, it originates from deep wounds in the soul most often caused by the lack of genuine fatherhood in the formative years of life. Second, the organized church has done little to recognize this disease of the soul and has actually fueled it by perpetuating service rather than sonship. The church must have servants to keep their programs functioning. Third, because of the lack of true fatherhood in the church, believers continue to operate as slaves to the church rather than as sons and daughters who *are* the church. I mean no disrespect to the organized church, but it is true.

For the orphan-hearted person, the concept of God is tainted by life experiences and disappointments. God is often viewed as a tyrant who demands to be pleased, and the belief is perpetuated that acceptance by God can only come through perfect performance and strict obedience. In the orphan's mind-set, acceptance and favor can come no other way.

Orphans have a limited capacity that focuses primarily on self. They are very narcissistic and the center of their own universe. They see others through a lens of rivalry, jealousy, and competition. Pastors and visionary leaders with this condition rule their ministries requiring strict loyalty and dispensing swift discipline toward those who do not follow the rules of the organization to the letter of the law. Because of being forced to make it in life on their own, orphans are very independent and self-reliant, causing them to be closed off, withdrawn, and distant in order to maintain control over their lives. Yet, in spite of this, orphans are starved for approval and affirmation through the praise and acceptance of others.

Orphan-hearted people are often chameleons who will change to become like those they admire, much like I wanted to become like Dr. Smitherman. Yet in spite of these changes, they constantly have a distorted self-image. They embrace a religious form in an attempt to change into an acceptable person, only to find that they cannot pray enough, give enough, or serve enough to reach the bar of acceptability. Since works can never supply the means by which the orphan-hearted can measure up, the lie is fed that they are cursed and must settle for a life of rejection, shame, and self-reliance.

**Healing of every soul is both
an event and a process.**

God *Has* Something Much Better

Healing of every soul is both an event and a process. While the initial breakthrough can be instantaneous, time and patience are required for healing to be completed. Healing the orphan heart is no different; it, too, is an event and a process. It begins when we recognize that we have an orphan heart and is completed when we come into the working knowledge that we are a son of God. So how do we do this?

We must begin by coming face-to-face with the truth regarding our condition and have the courage to face it and change it. It is not enough to recognize the presence of a disease in the soul; there must be genuine pursuit to be liberated at all costs. Recognition that our soul suffers from this infirmity is not enough. We must purpose to do whatever it takes to be free from its control.

We must start with repentance of all bitter-root judgments and forgive all who have deeply wounded our spirit and soul. This will release us from the curse of the orphan heart. For the record, not all curses are demonic spells. Curses can be any severe affliction. Many of us have been severely afflicted for years by the wounds of those who were supposed to love and protect, primarily fathers. The first step is the most difficult because it demands that we face our past with the greatest of courage, with purpose in our heart to be free, and with determination to never look back as we walk a new road of liberty.

Reset Your Identity

I enjoy movies. One of my favorites is *The Legend of Bagger Vance*. It is the story of a young man named Junuh who had a gift for golf. After winning an amateur competition, he enlisted in the Army in World War I. He became traumatized by the horrors of war and, as a result, lost his way in life. The character Bagger Vance is an angel sent to help Junuh find his way back to his identity and purpose in life; and, of course, the angel uses Junuh's gift of golf as the means to accomplish the assignment.

The tipping point in the movie comes when Junuh is at the brink of breaking free from his past but stalls out because the pain in his soul is too great. It is at this moment that Bagger says, "Ain't a soul on this entire earth ain't got a burden to carry he don't understand; you ain't alone in that. But you been carryin' this one long enough. Time to go on. Lay it down."

Junuh responds by saying he doesn't know how. Bagger replies, "You got a choice. You can stop. Or you can start walking."

Once again Junuh protests, "Where?"

Bagger responds, "Right back to where you always been. And then stand there. Still. Real still. And remember. Time for you to come on out the shadows, Junuh. Time for you to choose."

Junuh again protests, "I can't."

Bagger says, "Yes you can ... but you ain't alone. I'm right here with ya. I've been here all along. Now play the game. Your game. The one that only you was meant to play. The one that was given to you when you come into this world. Now is the time, Junuh."

Junuh hit the ball, a miracle shot, and ultimately regained his true identity and his purpose in life.

Could it be that many of us today are like Junuh? Have we been so wounded in life that we have lost our way and have no clarity of our identity and purpose? If so, the Son comes and says to each of us, "You have been carrying these wounds long enough. It is time to come out of the shadows and engage in the life that was intended for you to live from the day you were born." Only one who has been wounded can identify with another wounded soul. Jesus is a Savior who was willingly wounded in order that we could be healed of our wounds. He is the One who was "touched with the feeling of our infirmities" (Hebrews 4:15, KJV). He is the wounded Son who has come to heal the wounds of all the wounded sons of the earth. He not only understands our deepest wounds, but also provides the only way for us to walk freely from them.

Remember, in chapter 2, that Peter's identity was forever changed when he recognized Christ as "the Son of the living God" (Matthew 16:16). His life was never the same after that day. Having received a revelation that he was given a place in the Father's kingdom as a son, Peter saw himself as more than a fisherman. He was a son of the living God in Christ; that is, adopted into the family and given a seat in the Father's kingdom as a son! When Peter saw Jesus for who Jesus really was, Peter saw himself for who God had made him!

We must receive the revelation from Jesus that we are no longer orphans. In John 10:10, Jesus declared that His coming to the earth was to free men so that they might engage in the fullness of the life that God intended them to live. He is spoken of in Hebrews 2:10 as "bringing many sons to glory." He gave us the right to become "sons of God" (John 1:12, KJV) through His atoning work on the cross. I could go on, but the truth is clear. We are sons of the living God through the Son of the living God. We have been given a clear identity and the power to pursue the destiny and purpose in life for which we were ordained before being formed in our mother's womb. Our loving Father in heaven has removed the hurts and wounds of our earthly fathers. The Son, who willingly allowed Himself to be wounded, heals our wounds. What love is this!

Become Secure in the Father's Love

Many of us have heard about the love of the Father for so long and in so many sermons that we have tuned it out. The message falls on deaf ears. However, when the Father shows up in our darkest hour and restores our soul, we get a true revelation of this deep covenant love. Our discovery of His love usually comes when we are at our lowest in life. For David, that love was discovered in an entirely new level, both in the cave of Adullam, and following his sins of adultery and murder (Psalm 34 and Psalm 51, respectively). For the prodigal son, that love revelation came when he returned to his father in shame and disgrace, only to be received and restored to his purpose in life (Luke 15:11-32). For Peter, the message hit home after the resurrection when Jesus returned to him to affirm His love and set Peter on his life course (John 21:15-17). For me, the revelation of this love came when I wished to die; but God revealed His love and true Fatherhood to me instead.

**As a son we must know that our Father
does not demand perfection.**

As a son we must know that our Father does not demand perfection. Do we always want to do the right things in life? All of us do. Do we always do the right things in life? Not always. So then, does the Father love us less when we miss the mark and more when we hit it? Not in the least. So, why do we believe that we have to always do everything just right in order to win His favor? The answer: We are not secure in His love.

Not long ago, we conducted a conference on fatherlessness. As part of that meeting many of our men stepped up as fathers to minister to all in attendance who had been battling the orphan heart. I was amazed to see the change in many as the fathers prayed blessings over these precious orphans, declaring each one's sonship and reaffirming each one's value and worth to the Father in heaven. To each, the blessing of affirmation, love, and acceptance was released. There was also recognition and affirmation of each son and daughter's gifting, calling, and purpose in life. Destinies were set into motion. I could literally envision the shackles falling off the soul of each one who received ministry.

Dare to Trust Again

Proverbs 3:5-6 teaches us that we are to trust in the Lord with all of our heart, soul, and mind. We are not to depend upon our natural insight and understanding. These verses teach us that if we seek an intimate relationship with the Father through the Son and acknowledge the Lord, He will direct the course of our lives and make our destinies and purposes clear to us. The key element in this promise is to trust. In the Hebrew mind-set, trust speaks of being safe and secure as well as having a sense of well-being in one's soul. If we are living in a state of trust toward the Lord as our covenant Father, we are unconcerned about situations in life that appear to be uncertain. In short, when we truly trust our Father, our well-being is not governed or determined by the circumstances or events of life, whether good or bad.

Trusting the Father is not based upon our own merits or a tit-for-tat arrangement with the Father.

Trusting the Father is not based upon our own merits or a tit-for-tat arrangement with the Father, but rather founded upon His unwavering loyalty and glorious kindness to us, His offspring. Hope is not some type of mystical wishing upon a star, but rather a confident expectation of the goodness of our covenant Father. He can be trusted. Trust is no guarantee that we will live a stress-free life, but it does mean that we can find the place of peace and rest in the midst of the hardships and wars in our life because we know that our Father will see us through each obstacle to total victory. We can dare to trust the Father who loves us!

QUICK REVIEW – CHAPTER SIX

1. List three observations that the author has made regarding the orphan heart.

    a. _____.

    b. _____.

    c. _____.

2. Healing of the soul is both an _____ and a _____.

3. The key to healing the orphan heart is resetting _____ _____.

4. Why do we as believers think we have to do everything in life just right in order to have favor with God?

5. To what degree or level are you able to trust the Father with your life?

Chapter Seven

WE MUST HAVE FATHERS

For though you might have ten thousand instructors in Christ, yet *you do* not *have* many fathers; for in Christ Jesus I have begotten you through the gospel (1 Corinthians 4:15).

Ancient Corinth was one of the most commercialized cities of its day. Much of the shipping between the east and west passed through this great city; and with it, came multiple cultural influences that affected the populace. Corinth was renowned for its sensuality and sacred prostitution. According to history, the deity of the city was Aphrodite, the goddess of licentious love; and a thousand professional prostitutes served in the temple dedicated to her worship. Given the spiritual climate of the city, one can imagine the issues that arose within the church.

It is interesting to note that it was to this particular church that Paul addressed the need for spiritual fathers. There were many teachers who clearly taught doctrine; and the gifts of the Holy Spirit were, without a doubt, operating within the church structure. The anointing of God was present among the believers. Yet, in spite of this, there was an obvious absence of genuine fatherhood, and as a result, there were cultural issues that infected the body of believers. Paul recognized that these issues could only be resolved through proper spiritual parenting. Sadly, we see these same moral issues infecting the modern churches today. No doubt the need for true spiritual fatherhood is necessary today!

The word *fathers* in the above passage is *pateres* in the Greek and is translated *fathers, parents; those who are mature in the Lord.* It is a word derived from a root that means *nourisher, protector, and upholder; one who is advanced in the knowledge of Christ; one who stands in a father's place caring for the spiritual children.* *Pateres* speaks of those who have spiritual stature, stability, and wherewithal. The word does not speak of those who are most famous or have written the most bestselling books. *Pateres* also describes those who are grounded in the Word and the Spirit as well as those who are stable, wise, and not easily moved. It is the picture of those who govern and lead others to govern. Fathers and mothers are mature models for spiritual children to follow.

We are in a critical hour in God's church when the demands for fathers to step up and take their place in both the home and the church have never been more real.

John MacArthur writes, "What do tenderhearted mothers and loving fathers have in common? The motive that drives them is a desire for their children's maturity and well-being. A good father is no less self-giving than a nursing mother. But his role is different. The mother tenderly nurtures the infant; the father is the principal guardian and guide." There are commonalities and differences in the roles of the mother and father, yet the father has been given first responsibility to establish the identity and destinies of the children. We are in a critical hour in God's church when the demands for fathers to step up and take their place in both the home and the church have never been more real. The destinies of generations are at stake.

Qualities of Mature Fathers

Billy Graham has said, "A good father is one of the most unsung, unpraised, unnoticed, and yet one of the most valuable assets is our society." He further stated that the greatest quality of a godly father is to be present in the home. Consider these statistics from the IDS 302 Project [http://the fatherlessgeneration.wordpress.com] regarding education and the presence of the father in the home:

- Fatherless children are twice as likely to drop out of school.
- Children with fathers who are involved are 40% less likely to repeat a grade in school.
- Children with fathers who are involved are 70% less likely to drop out of school.
- Children with fathers who are involved are more likely to get A's in school.
- Children with fathers who are involved are more likely to enjoy school and engage in extracurricular activities.

There is something about the mere presence of a father that brings peace, security, and stability to the home. The same is true in the church. The presence of godly fathers in the house brings a notable level of security and stability to the body. Fathers seem to set the tone for the household of faith. When they demonstrate love for God and others, the impact is greater than we can imagine. Sons are deeply affected by this. Sons draw strength from a father's soberness and exhibit a high level of respect toward fathers who consistently and faithfully lead the congregation.

Fathers are those who have a unique relationship with their offspring. In 1 Corinthians 4:15, Paul made the comparison between instructor and father. *Instructor*, or *paidogoguos*, means *boy leader, tutor, or schoolmaster.* An instructor is simply one whose occupation is teaching. He is one who disseminates information and assists students in assimilating that information in order to put it to use. Fathers, on the other hand, are the ones who seek to transform children into mature sons by investing a deep personal impartation into their lives. They may teach, but their goal is not to simply have smart kids who are well learned. They want sons and daughters who are living in their full potential and pursuing their God-given destinies. Paul made it clear to the Corinthian believers that he was not their teacher; he was their father!

Encouragement

The father-heart in Paul was evident in his letters to his sons. He spoke of Timothy as "my dearly beloved son" (1 Timothy 1:2 KJV; 2 Timothy 1:2 KJV) and of Titus as "my own son after the common faith" (Titus 1:4 KJV). His heart for the sons and daughters of the faith was clearly seen in his epistles. He was constantly encouraging them to grow into full maturity. He acknowledged their identity, affirmed their value and worth, and spoke blessing over them. He prophesied over their destinies. He continuously made mention of them in his prayers as he interceded for the highest and best to be manifested in their lives. On more than one occasion, he prayed without ceasing for his spiritual offspring. Paul encouraged his spiritual children and, in so doing, set the example of spiritual fatherhood that we can follow today.

Remember, sons have permission to fail, and missing the mark does not make them failures.

Fathers recognize the gifts and strengths of their children and spend time developing them. They steward these gifts with patience and wisdom as the children grow and develop in maturity. They make sure that the gifts are tempered with love and grace so as not to be used selfishly or pridefully. By the same token, fathers are careful not to rebuke and penalize their children for failures or missteps in the development of their gifts. Remember, sons have permission to fail, and missing the mark does not make them failures. Fathers intervene to address weaknesses in spiritual children. They offer support and provide the means to strengthen the areas of weakness. Fathers do not overlook the weaknesses nor deny their existence. They simply recognize them and assist their offspring to overcome them and become spiritually healthy.

Fathers also encourage their offspring in practical life issues. Not everything in life is spiritual in nature. Some life issues require common sense and practical wisdom. Children commonly look to fathers for help in these matters, trusting that the fathers' wealth of experience will help them navigate a workable solution.

Impartation

Lester Sumrall was the very first spiritual father to release a blessing over my life. This blessing came at a time when I had no idea that there was such a thing. He sat with me, engaged me in deep conversation about my life, and then took my hand and prayed a blessing that remains with me to this day. His prayer was not a common, ritualistic prayer but rather a direct, pointed, and strategic prayer of blessing regarding my life and assignment. Within his prayer of blessing was a release of authority and power that could only have been orchestrated by the Father Himself. It was a blessing so profound I could not speak of it for days. It touched a deep place in my soul like nothing ever had.

A greater blessing came through my spiritual father, Apostle Jim Hodges. It occurred in a meeting with Apostle Jim and members of our ministry staff and family. We were working through personal issues that had arisen from a former ministry season. Each of us had served under a leader who had an orphan heart that created deep wounds in our souls. Dr. Don Crum, who was assisting Apostle Hodges, placed a coffee cup on the floor and asked each of us to symbolically place our wounds in that cup. Each of us placed our hurts and wounds into that cup. Then Dr. Crum performed a symbolic prophetic act. He took Apostle Jim's shoe, released a decree declaring Apostle Jim's authority over us as our spiritual father, and smashed the cup with the heel of that shoe. The cup did not just break; it exploded into pieces so small they could hardly be seen with the eye. Apostle Jim then pronounced to all of us in the room, "You are orphans no more!" We declared in unison, "We are sons!" The issue was settled in each of us forever.

Fathers are leaders both in the home and the church. It is hard work. Fathers are responsible for the care of the sons and daughters. True fathers care deeply about their offspring, not only in word but also in action. Just as natural fathers love to give to their children, spiritual fathers love to impart spiritual gifts to their spiritual sons and daughters. The Scriptures record that Moses imparted the spirit of wisdom to his spiritual son, Joshua (Deuteronomy 34:9). Elisha received a double portion of Elijah's mantle from Father God (2 Kings 2). Paul longed to see his spiritual offspring in order that he might impart some spiritual gift to them (Romans 1:11), and he activated the gift of faith in his spiritual son, Timothy, by the laying on of hands (2 Timothy 1:6). Jesus imparted the Holy Spirit into His spiritual sons, the disciples (John 20:22).

Impartation and fatherhood go hand in hand. Some impartations come through teaching; some come through ministry; but most come when fathers spend time with sons in spiritual matters. Just like my experience with Dr. Smitherman, I learned more by spending time and serving with him than through formal training. In fact, the majority of my learning has come in this manner. In my years of ministry training, I received much in the way of spiritual impartation by serving some wonderful men and women of God. The Holy

Spirit knows how to link us with spiritual fathers and mothers to get into us what is needed for our life assignment.

Protection and Correction

One of the major blessings of having spiritual fathers is protection. They carry in their hearts a deep desire to see their children grow to full maturity and become successful in their life assignments. They are very protective of anything that might come to stop or short-circuit that from happening. This is one of the hallmarks of genuine spiritual fatherhood.

Moses likened his assignment with the children of Israel to "a nursing father (who) beareth the sucking child" (Numbers 11:12, KJV). He was not only given the charge to lead the Israelites to the Promised Land, but was also given the responsibility for their safety and security as a loving, caring father. On one occasion when God wanted to destroy the entire nation and start over with Moses alone, this father of the faith stood in the gap for his children and admonished the Lord to "relent from this harm to Your people" (Exodus 32:12). Something rises up in the heart of a father to protect his offspring when they are in danger.

Protecting spiritual children is the work of correction. Timothy, who was a precious son to Paul, traveled and ministered with Paul and Silas on their missionary journeys. He was a well-respected young man and yet very timid. Timothy was sent by Paul to Thessalonica, Corinth, and Ephesus where he was assigned to deal with the false teachers, supervise public worship, and assist the church in setting in leaders. In the process of his assignment, Timothy encountered strong persecution and resistance from false teachers. In order to help his young son, Paul encouraged him and also corrected him. He told Timothy in 2 Timothy 1:7, "For God has not given us a spirit of fear, but of power and of love and of a sound mind." This was not a rebuke; it was a correction. Interestingly, Paul used the word "us" to let Timothy know that all great men of God encounter fear in their assignments, including Paul.

On another occasion, Paul encouraged Timothy to hit the reset button in his memory when he stated, "I put you in remembrance that you stir up the gift of God, which is in you by the putting on of my hands" (2 Timothy 1:6 KJV). In bringing correction, Paul also released encouragement. He knew that if Timothy would stop for a moment and remember the impartation that had come from his spiritual father, he could release the power of that impartation again into his current situation.

We can operate with our father's mantle while we are growing into our own.

There are times when I get bombarded with things that weigh down my soul. Sometimes the weights become so heavy that they are nearly impossible to bear. In these times, I remember that prayer of Lester Sumrall and the impartation he released into me. I not only recall it, but I draw the impartation into the present moment and find strength in my spirit that I thought was not there. There are also times when I am ministering and I recognize the need for a higher level of wisdom and apostolic authority for the situation. In those times, I literally recall the mantle and impartations that have been given into my spirit by my spiritual father, Jim Hodges.

In the Spirit, I literally put his coat upon my shoulders and his shoes on my feet and walk in the authority and anointing of his fatherhood over my life. We can operate with our father's mantle while we are growing into our own.

Correction and instruction from a spiritual father will help us stay on track with our ministry assignment and keep us stable in our private life, if we are willing to submit ourselves to it. I have known far too many ministers who became shipwrecked because they were unwilling to submit to a spiritual father. Their non-submission opened their souls to the orphan heart that destroyed their ministries and futures. Their followers often become shipwrecked as a result. We cannot afford to become another casualty!

Love *Is* the Glue

I conducted a wedding a number of years ago. It was a most special occasion that I was particularly honored to be a part. As the bride was walking down the aisle and the marriage covenant was about to be sealed, I heard the Holy Spirit say, "Love is the glue that will hold them together." I shared that word with those in attendance and then invited both families of the couple to surround them. Together, we released a prayer of blessing. It was a very powerful time, and that couple is thriving in their marriage and family to this day.

All who read the Bible know that love is the foundation of all covenant relationships (1 Corinthians 13). Without it, we all will fail. The love of the Father was clearly expressed through the Son who gave His life for all of us who will receive Him. Jesus said, "For God so loved the world that He gave His only begotten Son, that whoever believes in Him should not perish but have everlasting life. For God did not send His Son into the world to condemn the world, but that the world through Him might be saved" (John 3:16-17).

Love was the glue that held Him to the cross; love was the glue that sealed our covenant with the Father; and love remains the glue that holds any and all father-son relationships intact. The Father's covenant of love is open for all who will receive the Son and is reserved in fullness for all who do. His love covers a multitude of failures in life and is the fuel for redemption and restoration. We must allow this love to deliver us from the orphan heart and place us as sons into the fullness of our purposes and destinies in life.

The Possibilities

I cannot help but recall the introductory statistics that were reported by that news commentator regarding the fatherless epidemic in our nation:

- 71% of all high school dropouts come from fatherless homes.
- 75% of all adolescent patients in chemical abuse centers come from fatherless homes.
- Boys without both parents present are twice as likely to become gang members as boys with both parents present.
- 56% of all jail inmates grew up in a single-parent household or with a guardian.

We cannot afford for this trend to continue, much less grow!

What are the possibilities that these statistics could dramatically be altered by one simple change in our culture: the emergence of fathers? What difference would it make in our nation if genuine fatherhood would arise in the homes and the churches of our nation? How would the fathers' leadership and influence change the lives of generations? What would become of child sex trafficking, gangs, drug and alcohol abuse, and violent crime if the nation's offspring were spared the orphan heart syndrome by receiving their true identity as sons and daughters?

We can redeem the time and reverse the curse of fatherlessness in our spheres of influence.

We have a unique opportunity to redirect the course of history. We can redeem the time and reverse the curse of fatherlessness in our spheres of influence. We must never underestimate the authority and power that we have been given as fathers and mothers to shape the destinies of our offspring. For each son and daughter who knows his or her identity and purpose, there is one less orphan wandering aimlessly in life. We must assume our responsibility as fathers and mothers of the faith and shift the future of generations and the future course of the nation.

QUICK REVIEW – CHAPTER SEVEN

1. Differentiate instructors and fathers.

   a. Instructors _____.

   b. Fathers _____.

2. Billy Graham stated that the greatest quality of a godly father is _____
   _____.

3. List four functions of a true father.

   a. _____

   b. _____

   c. _____

   d. _____

4. The foundation of all father-son relationships is _____
   _____.

5. Who is your spiritual father?

QUICK REVIEW ANSWERS

Chapter One

1. Bondage – servitude, dependence, or the state of being a slave; one who is in a permanent relation of servitude to another, his will altogether consumed in the will of another.

   Adoption – to be placed into the position of a son.

2. The orphan heart is a learned behavior that becomes entrenched in the internal paradigm or mind-set.

3. The source of one's orphan heart is deep wounding of the soul, primarily from fathers.

4. The orphan-hearted person is one who is in great internal pain due to perceived loss.

5. The orphan-hearted person is in desperate search for love and acceptance.

Chapter Two

1. The two-fold revelation that Simon received in Matthew 16:16 was: 1) Jesus was the Christ, and 2) Jesus was the Son of God.

2. Servant – a slave, laborer, or bondman.

    Son – a builder of the family name.

3. a. Servants honor their masters by working; sons honor their fathers by being sons.

    b. Servants build relationships by performance; sons by love and trust.

    c. Servants are works oriented; sons are inheritance oriented.

    d. Servants strive to earn love; sons freely receive love.

    e. Servants are motivated by fear of punishment or hope of reward; sons are motivated by acceptance.

4. The need for fathers in the church today is overwhelming.

Chapter Three

1. Jesus was so passionate about sharing the Passover meal with His disciples before being crucified because He knew that a new covenant relationship was going to be established for them and all mankind for all eternity.

2. a. The best robe symbolized the father's covering and blessing.

   b. The ring symbolized the father's covenant with his son and the confirmation of the son's renewed authority.

   c. The shoes symbolized protection and the son's renewed ability to walk out his ordained destiny.

3. The older brother was upset with the celebration of his younger brother's return because he also had an orphan heart.

4. a. Babe – one who must be nurtured and constantly fed in order to be spiritually viable.

   b. Child – one who is not yet mature but in the process of becoming so.

   c. Son – one who is relationally mature and engaged in fulfilling destiny and purpose in life.

5. *Ben* is translated *builder, as one who builds the family name*

Chapter Four

1. Bitter roots are defined as sinful reactions to painful events.

2. Bitter roots express themselves as condemning judgments of people and also the refusal or inability to forgive those who have hurt us.

3. a. Cynicism

   b. Criticalness

   c. Apathy

   d. Negativity

4. The only way to remove a bitter root from our soul is to cut it at the root.

5. Removing bitter roots from our soul is through repentance of our condemning judgments and forgiveness of those who hurt us.

Chapter Five

1. To grow into the glory of sonship means to be transformed into the image and likeness of the Son of God Himself.

2. *Glory* is best described as the appearance, form, or aspect of a person which catches our attention and commands our recognition.

3. To "Kiss the son" means to respect, honor, and pay homage to the one who is superior.

4. Walking with the Son represents a covenant union whereby we begin as servants and grow into the true character and nature of the Son, Himself.

5. Sons not only know the Word of God, but also His ways.

Chapter Six

1. a. It originates from deep wounds in the soul most often caused by the lack of genuine fatherhood in the formative years of life.

    b. The organized church has done little to recognize this disease of the soul and has actually fueled it by perpetuating service rather than sonship.

    c. Due to a lack of true fatherhood in the church, believers continue to operate as slaves to the church rather than as sons and daughters who are the church.

2. Healing of the soul is both an event and a process.

3. The key to healing the orphan heart is resetting your identity.

4. As believers, we think we have to do everything in life just right in order to have favor with God because we are not secure in His love.

Chapter Seven

1. a. Instructors – tutors, schoolmasters, teachers.

    b. Fathers – nourisher, protector, upholder; one who stands in a father's place caring for the spiritual children.

2. Billy Graham stated that the greatest quality of a godly father was to be present in the home.

3. a. Encouragement – affirmation and stewarding the gifts, strengths, and weaknesses of the children.

    b. Impartation – releasing the blessing of the father over and into the children.

    c. Protection – being watchful over the children and looking out for their welfare.

    d. Correction – redirecting the children through love and instruction in truth.

4. The foundation of all father-son relationships is love.

About the Author

Larry Burden has been in full-time ministry for nearly thirty years. He founded his first church in Texas in 1987 where he served as pastor until relocating to California in 1992. There he and his wife Kathy attended Bible school and later joined the staff of a newly established church and international ministry where they served as associate pastors of the church, taught in the Bible school, helped build the ministry, and traveled domestically and internationally to minister the gospel of Christ.

The Burdens returned to Texas in 2000 where they founded Kingdom Life International Inc., in Frisco. They currently serve as pastors of Kingdom Life and are ordained through the Federation of Ministers and Churches International. Larry and Kathy are also ordained senior chaplains through International Fellowship of Chaplains (IFOC). Through the IFOC, they founded the IFOC Frontline Chaplain Corps in Frisco.

Larry's life assignment is to establish the kingdom of God in the hearts of all who will follow Jesus. His ministry blends the stability of the Word of God, the strength of the Holy Spirit, and the love of the Father to grow the family, to develop the army, and to release the true followers of Christ into their life assignments. His ministry is designed to shift the traditional church into the mind-set of the kingdom of God in order to genuinely impact society at every level for the glory of God.

Author Contact

Larry Burden welcomes the opportunity to speak at churches, conferences, and various business settings. For more information or to schedule Larry Burden to speak, please contact:

Larry Burden
Kingdom Life International Inc.
P.O. Box 1749
Frisco, TX 75034
214-618-1500
www.kingdomlife.org

AUTHOR PRODUCT

Additional copies of *The Orphan Heart* are available from your local or online bookstore, in e-book format, or directly from:

Larry Burden
Kingdom Life International Inc.
P.O. Box 1749
Frisco, TX 75034
214-618-1500
www.kingdomlife.org

ALSO AVAILABLE FROM LARRY BURDEN:

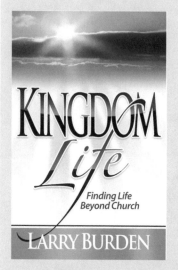

Paperback

138 pages

$11.99

This book is a must read for anyone in Christendom who is tired of their current church experience, has been burned by their church leadership, or wants to experience a fresh move of God in their life. In *Kingdom Life: Finding Life Beyond Church,* you will discover:

- Why current church models are failing in America.
- Why your church experience often leaves you empty inside.
- The true freedom and blessing that is found in the kingdom of God.
- How the kingdom model can genuinely change your life.
- How to restructure your current ministry model into one that expresses the kingdom.

This book is a must read for pastors, leaders, educators, marketplace ministers, and anyone seeking an effective kingdom model that will work in their ministry!